"Marine's poetry and art take the physical and show us the eternal values that lie just ben we may have forgotten to look for but whi beauty when we are shown them. This experience the world in a new way, and bring its magnificence freshly to your awareness."

~ **Dr. Allan Hunter**, Author of Gratitude and Beyond

"I began reading Marine's poetry book during a very busy morning... quickly, I was lulled into a gentle breeze which then sailed me into an ocean of love. The lyrical writing and prophetic prose captured my heart and gave me a glimpse into her powerful soul. Page after page I was captivated by her watery art so fluid and compelling that I lost myself in a heavenly home of oneness. Mahalo for turning a life altering adventure into a shared experience with all of us. I am honored and blessed to have participated in this experience."

~ **Faith Spina**, Bridge to Lemuria

"Marine creates endless waves of universal truths. The magic, enchantment and heartbeat of the ocean are here to lavish and nourish the reader. As a land-locked mermaid, I feel right at home, loved and secure. Enjoy."

~ **Sabrina Fritts**, Healer, Teacher and Friend. Contributing author of Speaking Your Truth, Courageous Stories from Inspiring Women, Volume III

"I felt transported to another world as I read Marine L. Rot's beautiful poems together with the beautiful watercolors on these pages. I highly recommend this book for all who seek further understanding of why we are here."

~ **Sierra Goodman**, The Divine Dolphin

"The physical beauty of Kauai is captured in the many moments of emotional beauty that become as you experience the islands treasures in these words. A simple way to say a simple thing to describe simple beauty. Marine captured the essence of the souls response to nature as it nurtures our souls."

~ **Nadia Khalil Bradley**, Author, Speaker and Teacher of Origination

"I have been on Kauai many times, so I know the powerful energy of the island and I can feel it on every page of this book. This book brings me back to this island because it is lit by Marine's love and infused with the magical energy of the island of Kauai."

~ **Baptist de Pape**, Producer of "the Power Of the Heart" movie

13.08.2013

Nara,
Dear Star Sister of Light,
Thank you so much for the High Frequency you emit through your Presence, sounds, words, and Motion.
I love you deeply.

From my Heart to yours,

♡

Marine Rot

KAUAI'S GIFT

POEMS INSPIRED BY AN ISLAND
AND LOVE FOR **LIFE**

WRITTEN AND ILLUSTRATED BY
MARINE L. ROT

Copyright © 2013 Marine L. Rot. All rights reserved.
Cover design, texts and illustrations: copyright © 2013 Marine L. Rot.
Edited by Naia Leigh

Love this book?
Order your autographed copy on:
www.marinerot.com

Kauai's Gift is also available on:
www.amazon.com

No part of this book may be reproduced or transmitted in any form or by any means,
electronic or mechanical, including photocopy, recording, or by any information storage
and retrieval system without the written permission of the author.
The author cannot be held responsible for any loss, claim,
or damage arising out of the use, or misuse of the content of this book.

Published 7/2013 by Marine L. Rot
marine@marinerot.com

ISBN: 1489526587
EAN-13: 978-1489526588

CONTENTS

Intoduction 9

Index of poems:

Where the river meets the ocean 10

Walking Tree 12

All is here 14

Happy for no reason 16

Sacred Dance 18

The dormant dream 20

It is written 22

See 24

Mantra of One voice 26

PerFICTION 28

Simple Bliss 30

A new being emerging 32

Goddess Pele 34

Mystic blue 36

Star Fruit 38

Breathe 40

Ocean of Love 42

This moment 44

Infinity 46

A note to you, reader 48

Mahalo 50

SPECIAL THANKS

This book is dedicated to my partner, husband, lover, best friend and teacher, Jernej, for his unconditional love and support. And to the Ocean, that gifted me with myself.

INTRODUCTION

I have always had a special connection with the ocean, although had yet to be fully aware of its preciousness until just recently. It all started on the day of my birth, when my parents gifted me with my name, Marine. I was a baby of the sea. I had been given deep blue eyes in which were painted the emotional states every passing moment. Vivid and magnetic these eyes, whether filled with immense joy, or a state of meditative contemplation, when turning blue-grey, are a reflection of my soul, a vessel on the ocean.

Water. Water is a blend of my greatest love and greatest fear. This became exceedingly so after I abruptly met life through death during a Near-Death Experience on the north shore of Kauai, Hawaii. In that moment I accepted everything. All happenings, all of me, all there is. This trip of a lifetime has given me a true sense of my own existence, my whole life experience, and has brought together the pieces of a great and mysterious puzzle. The poetry you are about to read is the transmission of this fantastic heart-opening journey. I thank you for holding this book in your hands and hope you enjoy it as much as I enjoyed writing and illustrating it.

Marine

WHERE THE RIVER MEETS THE OCEAN

Where the river meets the ocean,
I find myself crying to God.
So much beauty...
Thank you for this gift.

Where the river meets the ocean,
I find myself crying to God.
So much fear...
Thank you for this gift.

Where the river meets the ocean,
I find my love and my lust,
my light and my shadow,
my joy and my sorrow.

Where the river meets the ocean,
water flowing within herself,
diving and flying,
floating and surfing.

Seeing her full integration
into this communion.

WALKING TREE

Walking tree,
what are you running from?
Walking tree,
where are you coming from?

Looking for the essential form,
life is no boredom.
Surrender to your freedom.
Here is your true home,
being born
with no form.

Here is your time to come.
Home sweet home
Om
Omnipresent
O so potent
Om.
Sound of freedom,
Home.

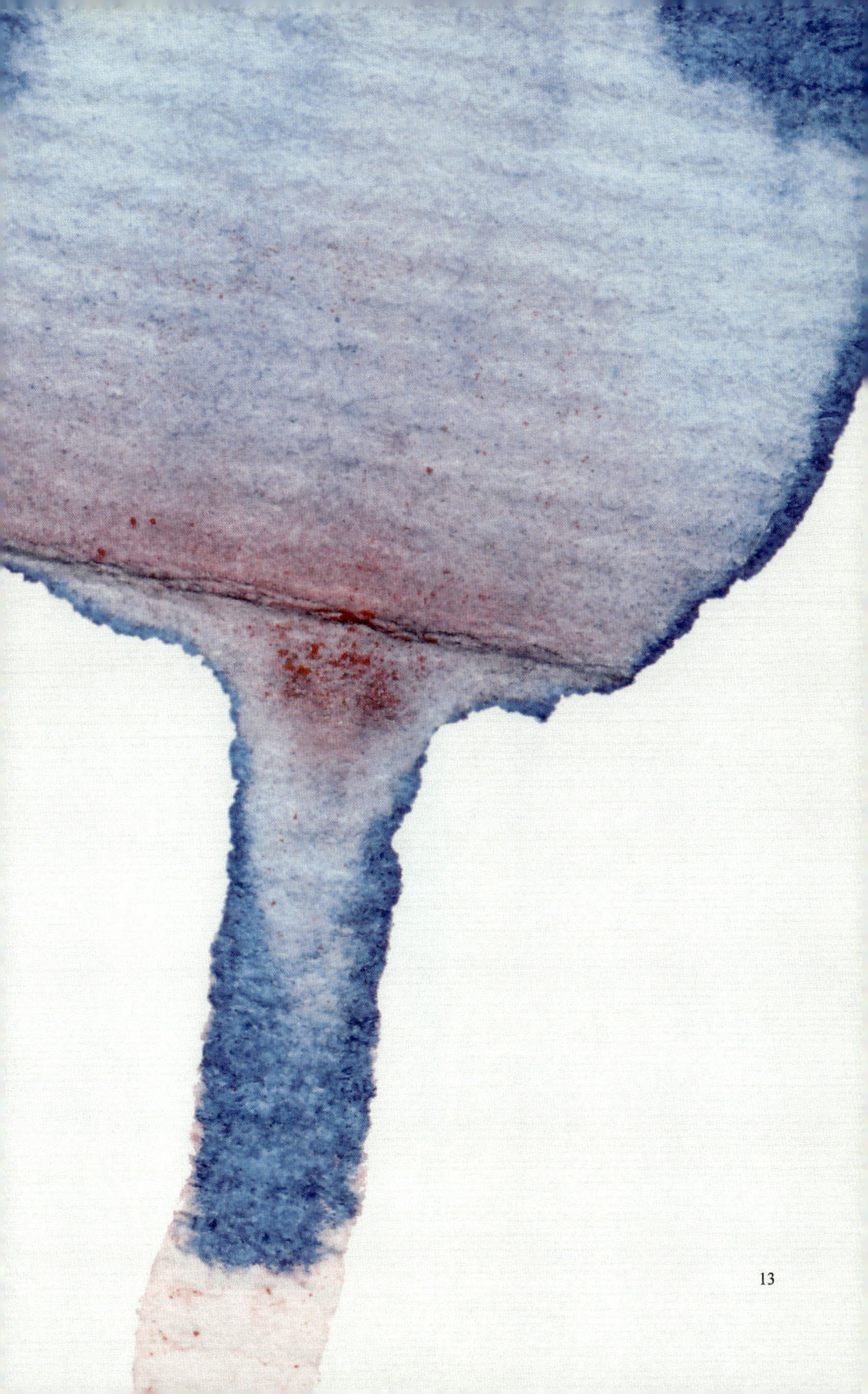

ALL IS HERE

All is here
for you to see,
for you to be.

The treasure is waiting for you,
right in front of you
or just behind the leaf.

Are you ready to perceive?
Are you ready to receive?

Always will it be here for you.

HAPPY FOR NO REASON

Happy for no reason,
is it reasonable?
In between art of faith
and tree of possibilities
is laying this ecstatic dance of life
that we are.
This,
is the perfect orchestration
to be happy
for no reason.

SACRED DANCE

Thank you
for
any,
every,
everything.

Thank you for loving, chanting, dancing.
Cuddling, connecting, remembering.

Thank you for doubting.
Thank you for questionning.

And sometimes not understanding.

Thank you for being
part of life's sacred dance.

THE DORMANT DREAM

The dormant dream
has awakened me
from the dream
inside the dream.
Confirmation.
Ding!

IT IS WRITTEN

Children of the world,
children of the sky,
reunite and yet don't know why.

Children of the Earth,
children of the stars,
such a divine orchestration we are!

It is written in the sand,
it is written in the sky.
Master A, wizard of the blue,
stepping into divine creation.

Mandalas of love
beaming out of the new.

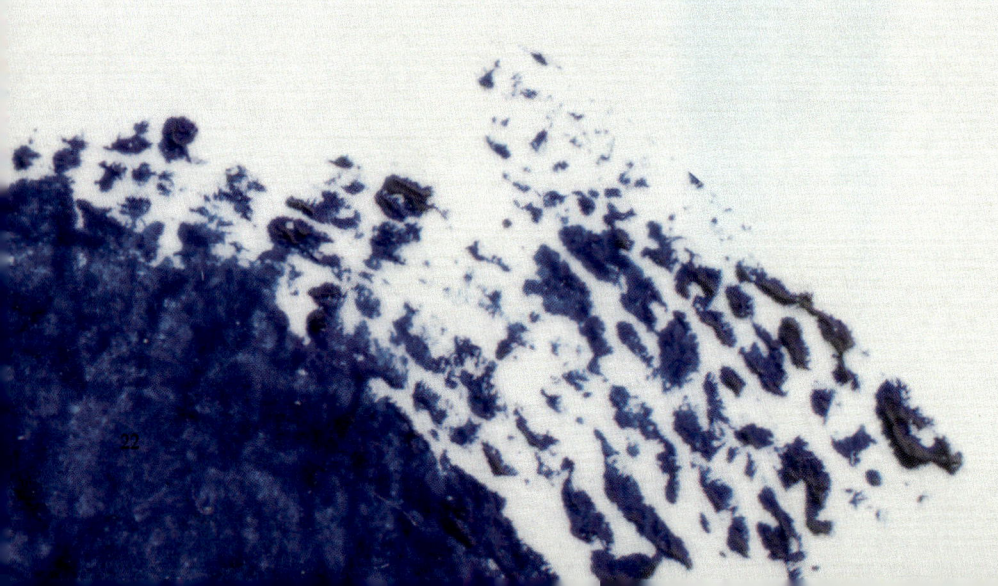

SEE

During those waves of surrender,
close your eyes and see.
Close your eyes and wait,
til your infinite patience

comes.

Close your eyes and see
what you have come to realize.
Always has been here
your true paradise.

MANTRA OF ONE VOICE

Our voices are chanting,
colorfully dancing
in the dark sky balancing,
embracing
it all.

Our sounds are dancing,
vibrations enlacing,
ribbons of ancient wisdom connecting,
resonance finally blending
into one and only
Being.

"PERFICTION"

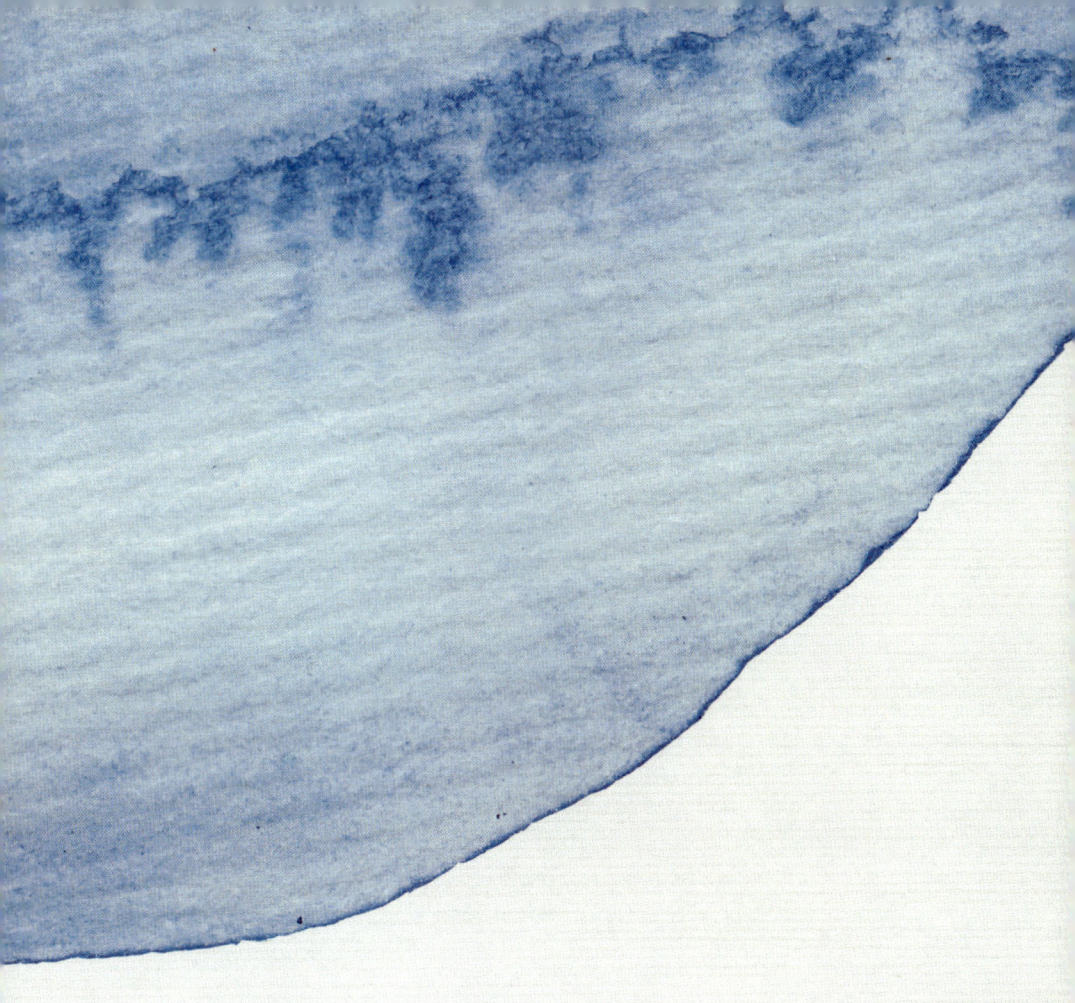

Perfect.
Perfect fit.
Perfect.
Perfection.
Indeed! Is this Perfiction?
So pure is this space,
so splendid is this time,
that for the Mind,
it all seems a Fiction.
Yet another sun is rising
With the same sound of
Perfection.

SIMPLE BLISS

No coffee please!
Only coconut bliss.
No caffeine please!
Better a gentle kiss.

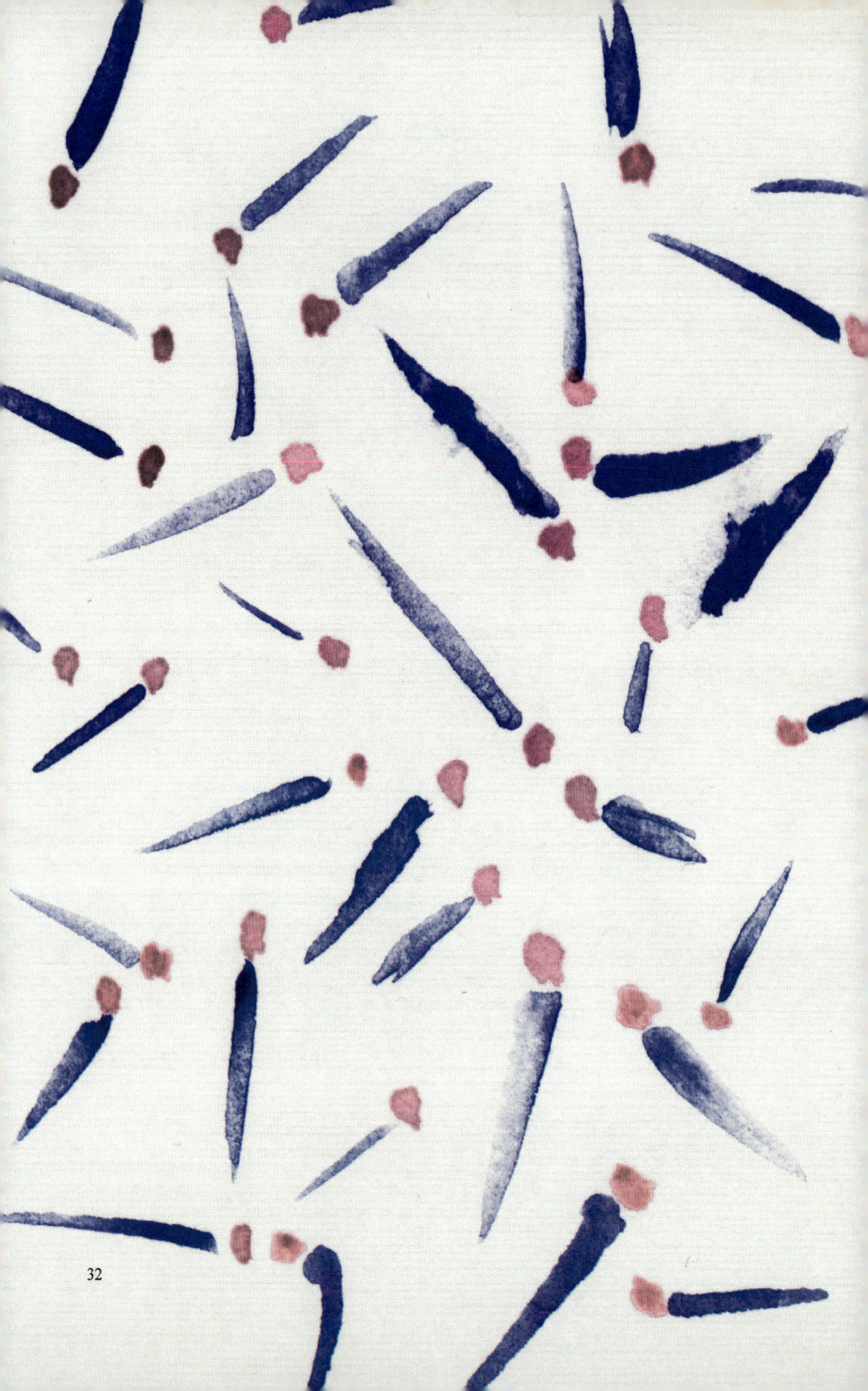

A NEW BEING EMERGING

Crystals in my scar,
in the shape of a heart,
have come to reunite me with my star,
the one I have been longing for, so far.
Smiling moon,
knowing,
out of the blue,
loving.
The new gradient of silver blue,
shining.

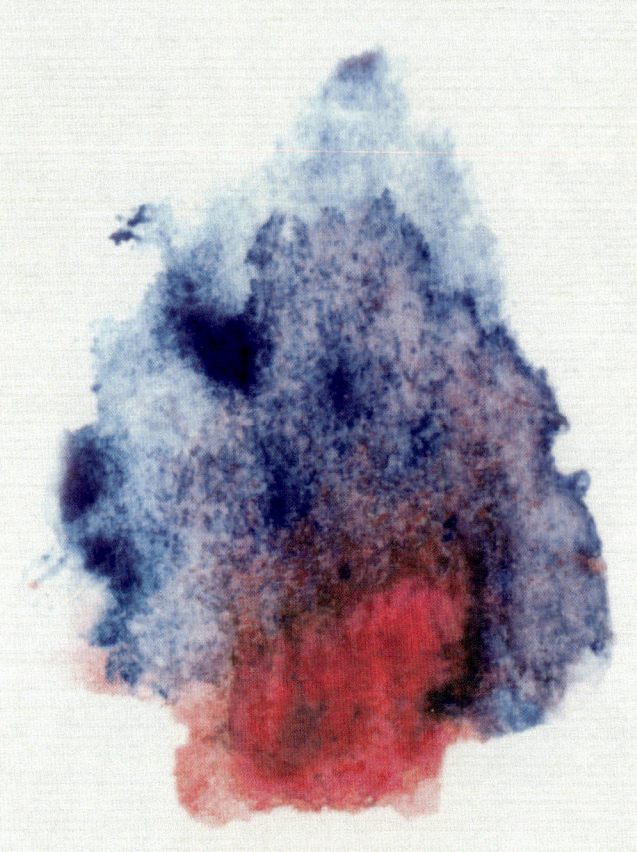

GODDESS PELE

Goddess Pele,
Red and Blue,
I honor your divine Trust.
I honor your Challenges.
Magnificent
Lava in the Ocean,
Fire in the Water.
Drops of Heat.
Tears of Joy.
O Holy Mountain of Wholeness!
What a colorful Dress!
Please and Thank you,
For offering me your Hand.

MYSTIC BLUE

Mystic blue,
crystal light,
slow motion.
Space for creation.
Sound and intention.
No room for the reason,
but intuition.
Gift of the day: Hanalei Bay.

STAR FRUIT

Another perfect day.
How are you today?
Star fruit of the Universe,
thank you for your juice.
Acid is a part of the palette
That somehow sweetens my palate.

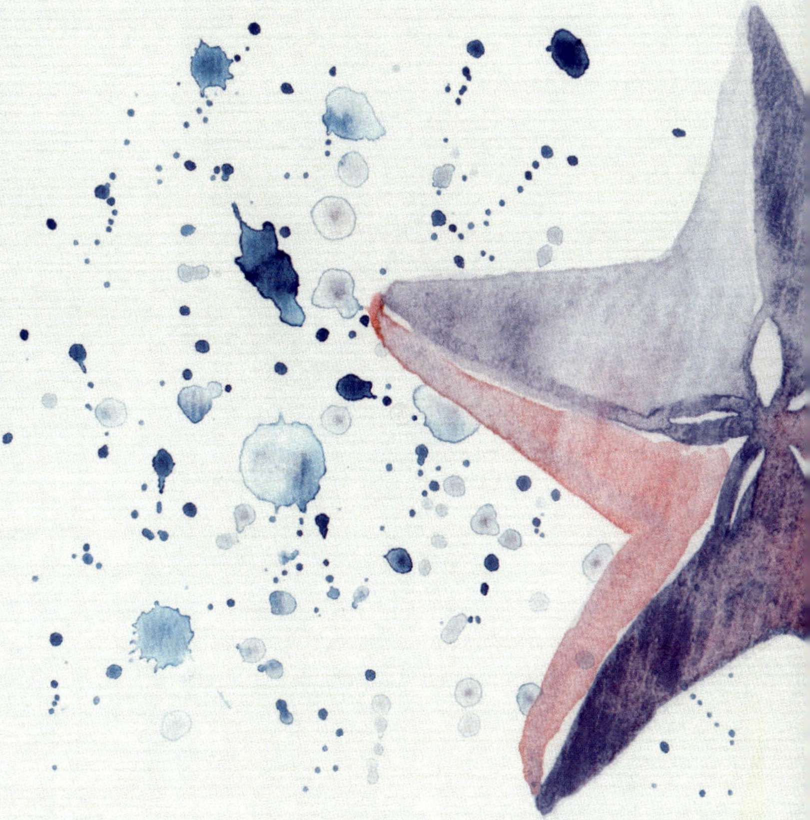

BREATHE

The shield on your breast
is holding upon your chest.
Listen to the gentle breeze
calling you to ease.
Breathe. Breathe.
Look how easy it is.
Breathe. Breathe. Breathe!
Breathe it in and out.
Give and you shall receive
the breath of life.

Any punishment is a derision.
Waterfall of love is my true mission.

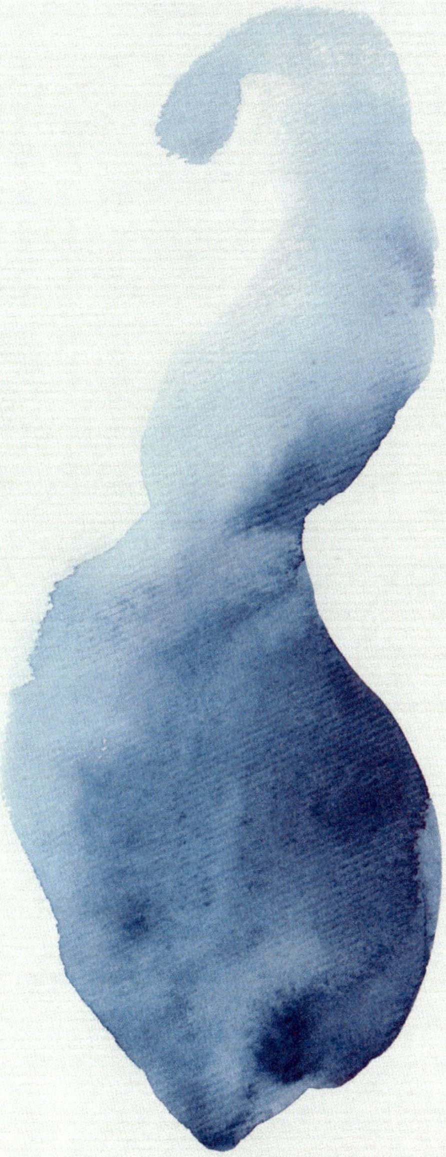

OCEAN OF LOVE

Once upon no time,
lived a little girl in the Ocean.
What a blessing
to grow in this environment!
In the middle of the Ocean,
Love is all there is!
Whales and dolphins,
algues and fishes,
and stones.
All emitting waves of Love.
Any doubt? Not a drop!
Because in the middle of the Ocean,
It all returns to Love.

THIS MOMENT

You know this feeling
of being in love…
with everything.
If you ever lose it,
remember.
Dance, sing, nurture,
kiss.

Embrace the moment.
Let your senses dive
into the gift of the day,
the beauty of Now.
Scents, colors, sounds,
touch.

The infinite palette of love.

No label, no expectation.
No "but", no "should", no "why".
For a moment,
relax.

In this moment,
find out that this
is the only thing you want for yourself
and for others.

INFINITY

**Infinity and Divinity
Here is my Serenity**

A NOTE TO YOU, READER

I am very grateful for the opportunity to connect with you, adventurer and Lover of Life. Aware of it or not, we hold many golden keys for one another. As we change, evolve, and grow, we sometimes forget about our unique inner gifts. Then, synchronistically, someone crosses our path offering their perception and reminds us of our own uniqueness; of the essential part we are here to play, and the beautiful talents we are here to share. There is a profound magnificence in each of one of us that decodes Creation's puzzle by bringing our own individual piece. Life is a Divine canvas ready to be painted, a book to be written, a stage to be performed on... the open space for infinite creation. And you are invited.

MAHALO

Mahalo to my Kauai Ohana, who made
and continues to make this journey
the most precious:

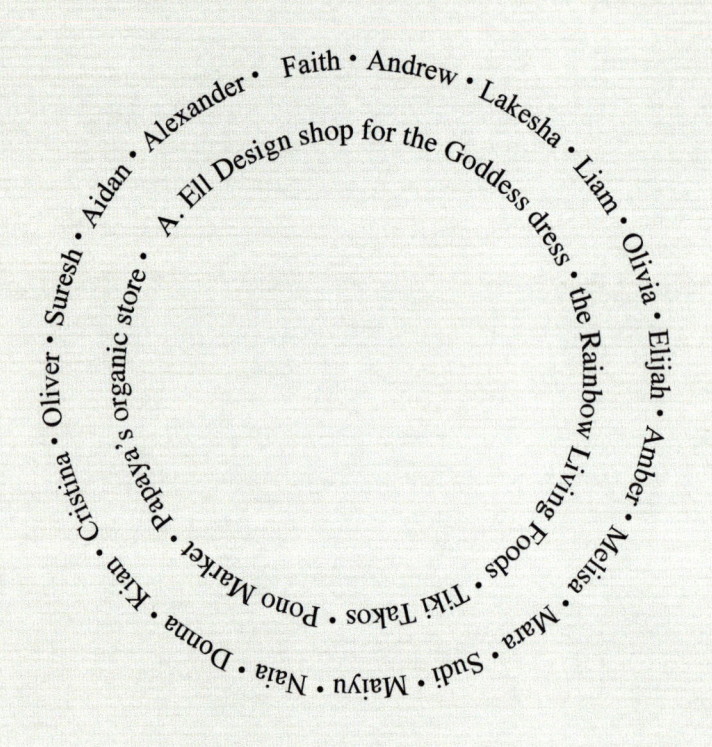

Aidan • Alexander • Faith • Andrew • Lakesha • Liam • Olivia • Elijah • Amber • Melisa • Mara • Sudi • Maiyu • Naia • Donna • Kian • Cristina • Oliver • Suresh

A. Ell Design shop for the Goddess dress • the Rainbow Living Foods • Tiki Takos • Pono Market • Papaya's organic store

MarineRot.com

Made in the USA
Charleston, SC
16 July 2013